The Story of THE BERMUDA TRIANGLE

by Noah Leatherland

Roar! Books, an imprint of Bearport Publishing by FlutterBee

Credits
Cover and title page, © Mark Bond/Adobe Stock and © adiba/Adobe Stock; 4, © Billion Photos/Shutterstock; 5, © Fer Gregory/Shutterstock; 6MR, © pkproject/Adobe Stock; 6M, © Nejron Photo/Shutterstock; 7, © Madelein Wolfaardt/Shutterstock; 8–9, © mozZz/Adobe Stock; 9, © Sarfaraz82/Shutterstock; 10ML, © Dimedrol68/Shutterstock; 10–11, © DEA/G. Dagli Orti/Getty Images; 11TR, © Public Domain/Wikimedia; 11M, © StockPhotoPro/Adobe Stock; 12, © Sarfaraz82/Shutterstock; 12–13, © US National Archives; 14M, © Sarfaraz82/Shutterstock; 14BR, © US Navy/Wikimedia; 15, © US Navy/Wikimedia; 16, © zelvan/Shutterstock; 16–17, © Chronicle/Alamy Stock Photo; 17, © Sarfaraz82/Shutterstock; 18, © MasPix/Alamy Stock Photo; 18–19, © bkkillustrator/ Shutterstock and © AI Creatives Studio/Adobe Stock; 20, © PintoArt/Shutterstock; 20–21, © Kostiantyn Komarov/Shutterstock; 22–23, © Parilov/Shutterstock; 23, © Rashmi Bharani/Shutterstock; 23BR, © Dennis/Adobe Stock; 24–25, © Benny Marty/ Shutterstock; 25, © Sarfaraz82/Shutterstock; 26–27, © Me dia/Shutterstock; 27, © Philip Schubert/Shutterstock; 28–29, © Alexandra Tyukavina/Shutterstock; 29, © BRA_Stk/ Shutterstock; 30, © Juice Flair/Shutterstock; 31, © Daniel/Adobe Stock

Bearport Publishing Company Product Development Team
Kayla Eggert, Theresa Emminizer, Kim Jones, Allison Juda, Naomi Reich, Steve Scheluchin, Tiana Tran

A Note on Colorization
Some of the historic photos in this book have been colorized to help readers have a more meaningful and rich experience. The color results are not intended to depict actual historical detail.

Library of Congress Cataloging-in-Publication Data is available at www.loc.gov or upon request from the publisher.

ISBN: 979-8-89577-841-8 (hardcover)
ISBN: 979-8-89577-849-4 (ebook)

For more information, write to Bearport Publishing, 3500 American Blvd W, Suite 150, Bloomington, MN 55431. Printed in the United States of America.

CONTENTS

HISTORY'S MYSTERIES

Most stories have a beginning and an end. However, some of them leave behind more questions than answers.

These tales have missing information or unlikely endings.

People have tried to solve famous mysteries for many years. Despite their efforts, parts of some of these stories remain unexplained.

Are you ready to explore a mystery?

THE MYSTERY OF THE BERMUDA TRIANGLE

The ocean covers 71 percent of Earth's surface. It still holds many mysteries that we haven't uncovered.

Because the ocean is so big, things can easily get lost in the waves. In fact, hundreds of ships and airplanes have gone missing at sea.

Some people believe there is a mysterious force that traps ships and airplanes in one region of the ocean. This place is called the Bermuda Triangle.

Many **myths** surround this area. But what exactly is the Bermuda Triangle?

THE TRIANGLE

More than 50 ships and 20 airplanes have disappeared in the Bermuda Triangle.

NORTH AMERICA

Atlantic Ocean

Gulf of Mexico

The Caribbean

Caribbean Sea

Pacific Ocean

This area is a part of the North Atlantic Ocean. It can be found near the Caribbean and the East Coast of the United States.

The three corners of the triangular region can be found in Bermuda, Florida, and Puerto Rico.

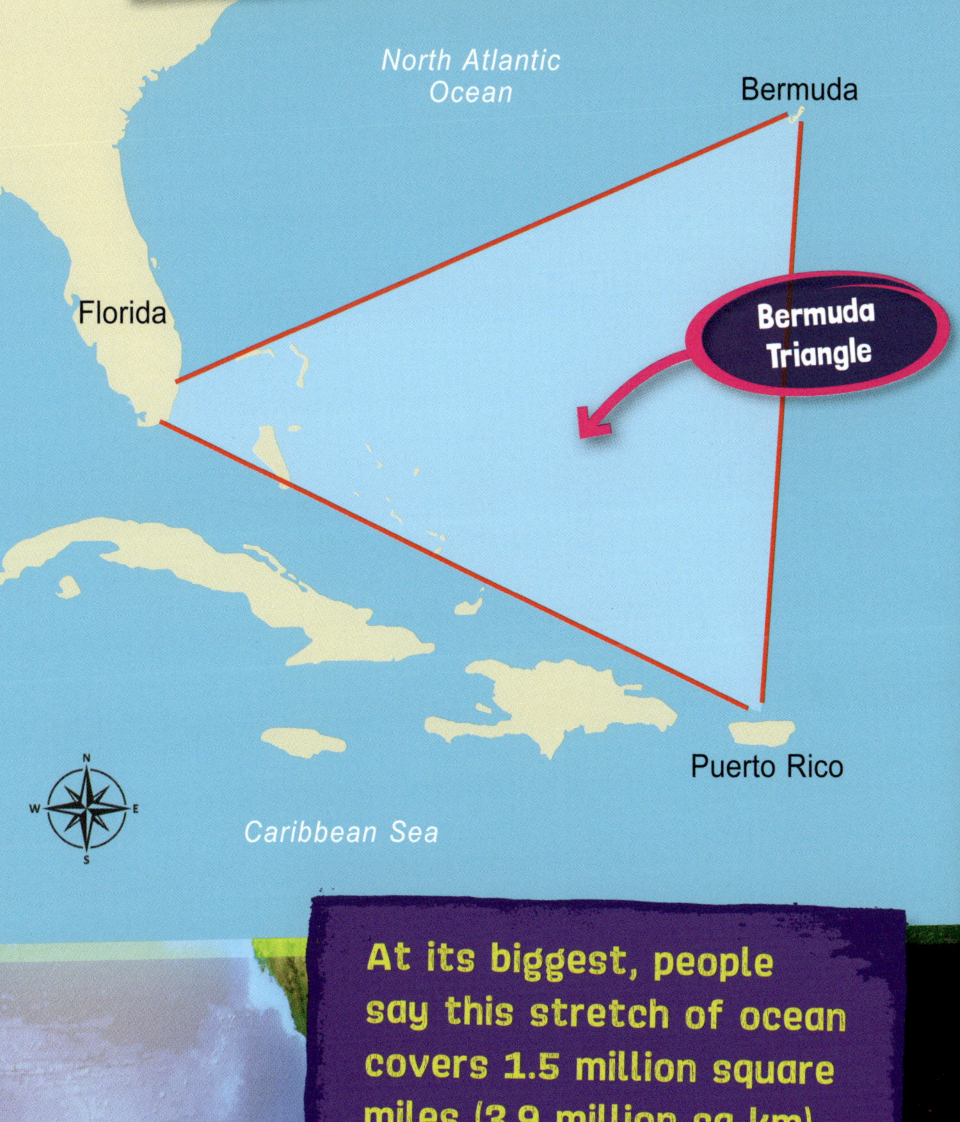

At its biggest, people say this stretch of ocean covers 1.5 million square miles (3.9 million sq km).

THE MYSTERY BEGINS

One of the earliest reports about the Bermuda Triangle dates back to 1492. Explorer Christopher Columbus wrote about strange compass readings here. He also described a large ball of fire falling into the sea while he traveled through this area.

Then in 1950, Edward Van Winkle Jones wrote an article about odd happenings in the region. This was the first time someone brought the mystery to the attention of the public.

In 1964, Vincent Hayes Gaddis wrote another article. He was the first person to give this region the name the Bermuda Triangle.

Vincent Hayes Gaddis

Vincent suggested that the disappearances of the ships and planes could be connected. People wondered whether the Bermuda Triangle was to blame.

THE USS CYCLOPS

In March 1918, a military ship called the USS *Cyclops* set off from Brazil. It was headed toward Baltimore, Maryland.

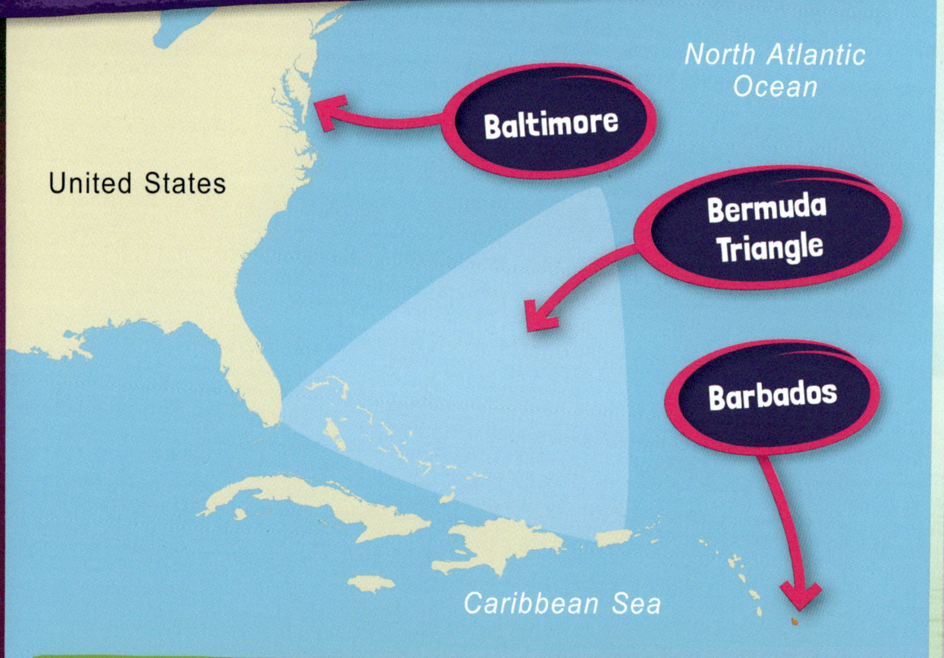

Along the way, the *Cyclops* stopped in Barbados. The ship left a message that all was well before taking off once more.

After that, the *Cyclops* was never seen again. No survivors or **wreckage** of the ship was ever found.

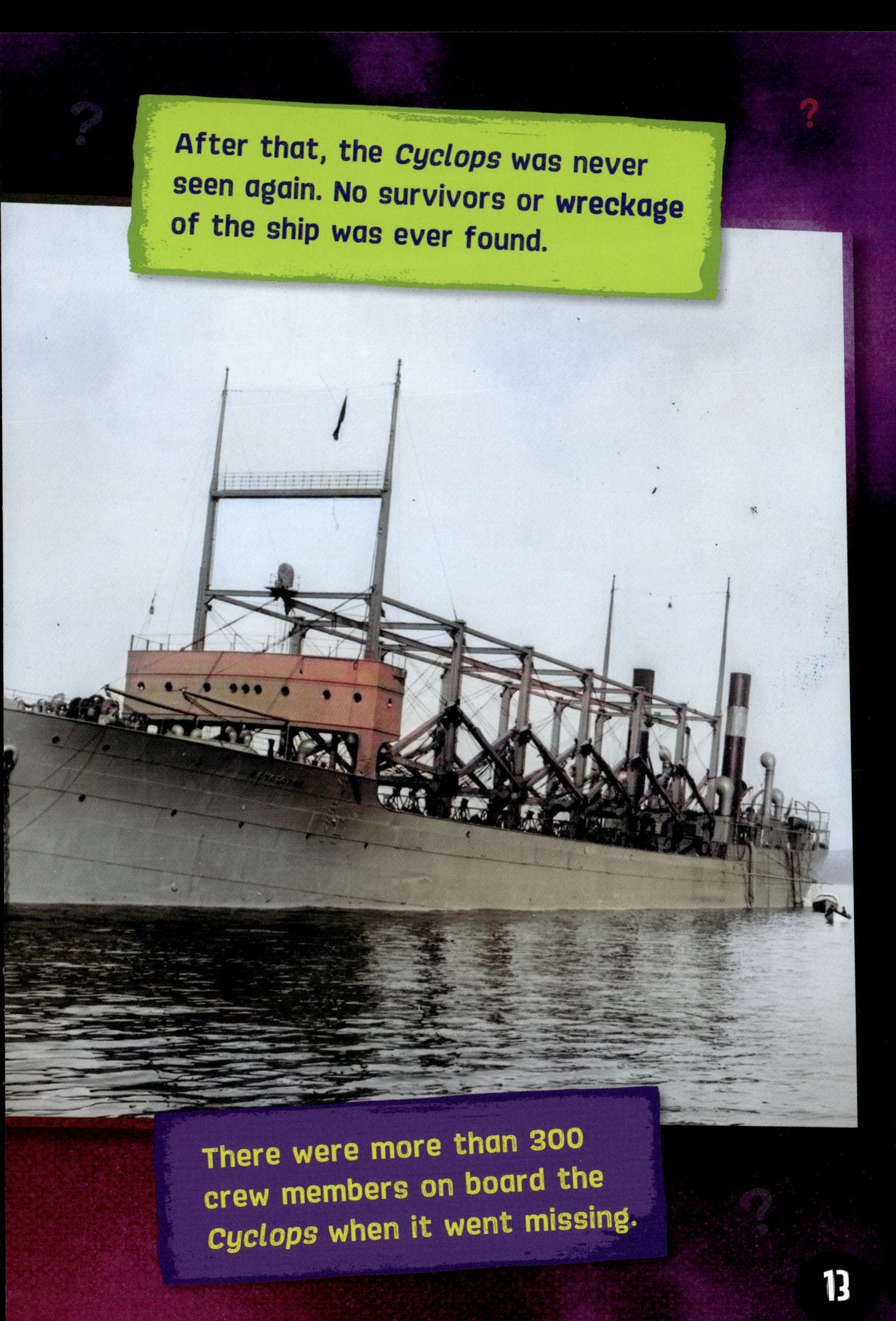

There were more than 300 crew members on board the *Cyclops* when it went missing.

FLIGHT 19

Another major disappearance occurred in December 1945. A group of five U.S. Navy planes went on a mission. Lieutenant Charles Carroll Taylor was in charge of the group, called Flight 19.

Charles Carroll Taylor

The planes left from Fort Lauderdale, Florida. They were to head out to the Bahamas, turn around, and come back. But along the way, something happened.

Air bases nearby picked up radio calls from Flight 19, asking for help. They sent search planes to look for the group.

A search plane

Despite their best efforts, the rescue planes couldn't find Flight 19. And while they were looking, one of the search planes went missing as well.

MISSING STARS

Mysteries surrounding the Bermuda Triangle continued. In January 1948, the *Star Tiger* took off from Santa Maria, Azores. It was headed for Bermuda . . . but the plane never made it.

No wreckage was found. Nor were any of the 31 people who had been traveling on the plane ever seen or heard from again.

Then, in January 1949, it happened again. The *Star Ariel* was flying between Bermuda and Jamaica. Somewhere in the Bermuda Triangle, it went missing.

North Atlantic Ocean

Bermuda

Florida

The Bermuda Triangle

Jamaica

Caribbean Sea

The planes disappeared almost exactly one year apart. And to this day, people still wonder what happened.

DIFFERENT THEORIES

What could be causing all of these disappearances? There are a few supernatural **theories**.

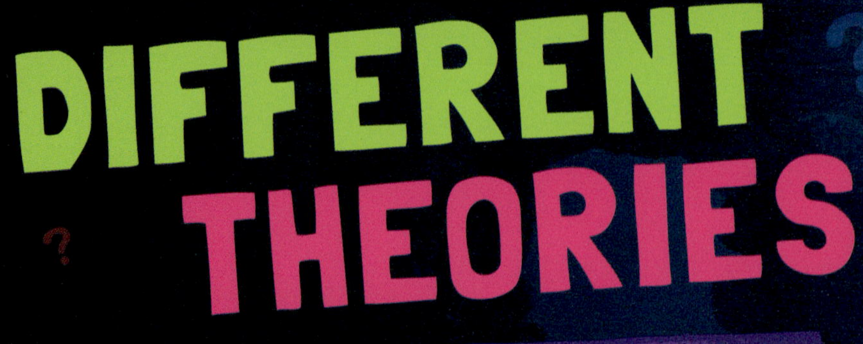

Some people blame something not from our planet. They think **aliens** are responsible.

Other people believe the disappearances are connected to the lost city of Atlantis. Like the city, they think planes and ships were swallowed up by the Bermuda Triangle.

Another theory says that the Bermuda Triangle sends things into another world. That's why nothing is ever left behind.

COMPASS PROBLEMS

One famous myth about the Bermuda Triangle involves compasses. It says that compasses work differently there, which makes people get lost.

Compass needles are naturally drawn to Earth's magnetic field. The direction in which the needles always point is called magnetic north.

Magnetic north is not a fixed point. It slowly changes over time, so compass users have to adjust their navigation.

When in the Bermuda Triangle, some people believe that compasses point to a fixed point called true north. If people don't account for this, they could get lost.

GOBBLED BY GAS

Gas could be another possible explanation. One theory says there is a lot of methane in the waters of this area.

Methane frozen in ice

Methane is let out when things decompose. Lots of methane can build up underwater.

Methane comes to the surface in bubbles. If a lot of these bubbles rise at once, they could unsettle a ship. This could make the ship sink.

The gas is very flammable. If it rose up to an airplane, a spark in the plane's engine could light it on fire. The plane may explode out of the air.

ROUGH ENVIRONMENT

Most people say that weather is behind the Bermuda Triangle disappearances.

Lots of storms and hurricanes move through this area. Extreme weather can make it very dangerous for planes and ships to travel.

And some people believe the strong Gulf Stream ocean current moves along any remains of planes and ships damaged in storms.

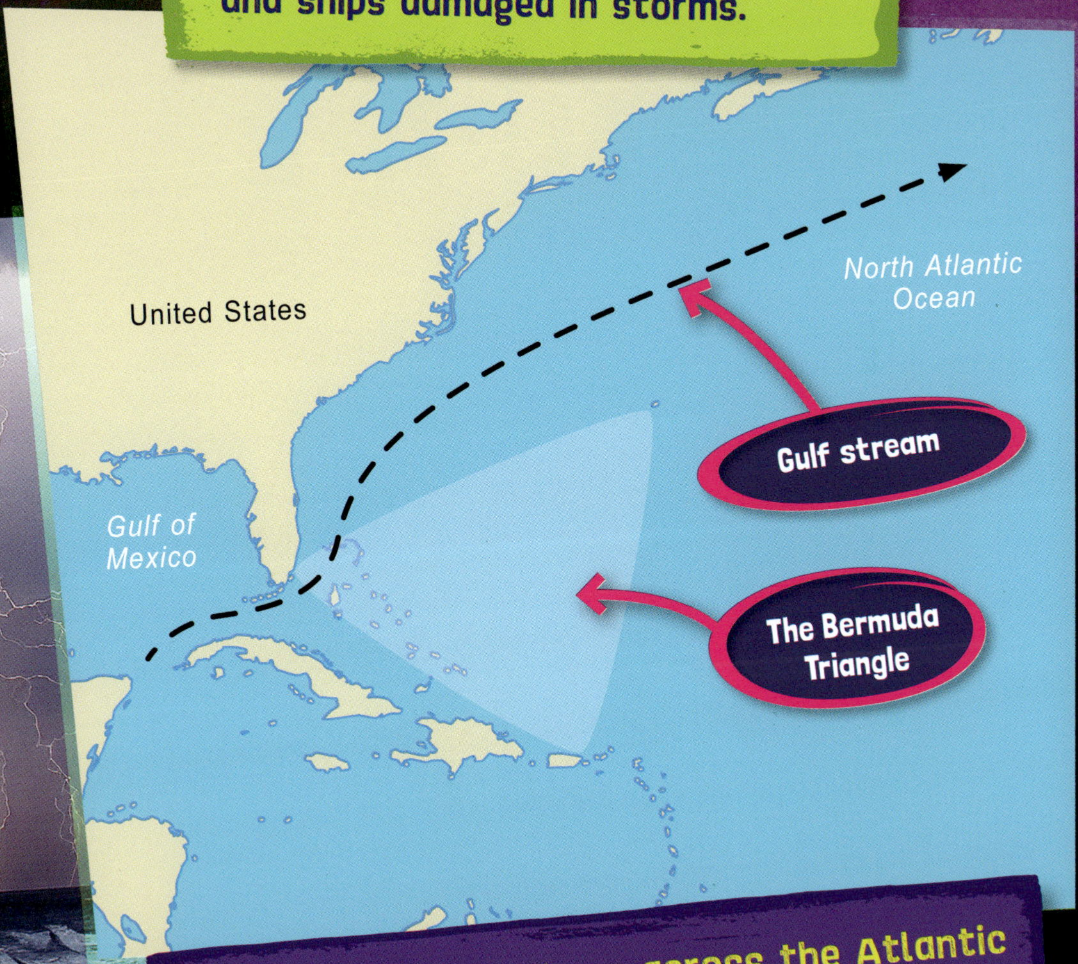

United States

North Atlantic Ocean

Gulf stream

Gulf of Mexico

The Bermuda Triangle

The Gulf Stream flows across the Atlantic Ocean, traveling along the East Coast of the United States and Canada. It could carry things thousands of miles away.

THE BERMUDA TRIANGLE TODAY

Despite all the stories and mysteries, the Bermuda Triangle is not marked on world maps. It is not recognized as an official region.

People and things still get lost in the Bermuda Triangle. However, the same can be said for other ocean regions.

Today, ships and planes still continue to travel through the area. It is one of the busiest parts of the ocean for transporting goods.

Luckily, the Bermuda Triangle is easier to travel through now. Navigation systems have improved. They allow people to know exactly where they are at all times.

FACT OR FICTION?

Many stories surrounding the Bermuda Triangle have not been explained. People still have many questions. What are people asking?

Why is wreckage never found? Powerful currents and strong storms could wash it away.

Did the disappearances have to do with Atlantis? No, Atlantis is a myth created by the ancient Greek philosopher Plato.

A lot of claims about the Bermuda Triangle are not true. However, the ocean is a large and unknown place.

Who knows what might be out there?

THE TRUTH IS OUT THERE!

There are plenty more clues we might yet uncover to solve the mysteries of the Bermuda Triangle. One day, we might get a step closer to discovering the truth.

It is fun to read about mysteries and wonder about what might have happened. What would you like to explore next?

GLOSSARY

aliens beings from another world

current a steady flow of water in one direction

decompose to rot or break down

magnetic field an area around a magnet in which magnetism flows

myths stories that often tell of mysterious events

navigation the act of following a route

philosopher a person who studies the nature of knowledge, reality, and life

theories ideas used as possible explanations for things that are not fully known

wreckage pieces that remain after something has been badly damaged

Index

Read More

Deniston, Natalie. *Bermuda Triangle (Do You Believe?).* Minneapolis: Jump!, Inc., 2025.

Harder, Megan. *Inside the Bermuda Triangle (Top Secret).* Minneapolis: Lerner Publications, 2023.

Williams, Dinah. *Bermuda Triangle (Unsolved).* New York: Scholastic Inc., 2025.

Learn More Online

1. Go to **FactSurfer.com** or scan the QR code below.
2. Enter "**Bermuda Triangle Story**" into the search box.
3. Click on the cover of this book to see a list of websites.